EVERGREEN

KIRSTEN ROBINSON

THOUGHT
CATALOG
Books

THOUGHTCATALOG.COM
NEW YORK · LOS ANGELES

THOUGHT CATALOG Books

Copyright © 2019 Kirsten Robinson. All rights reserved.

Published by Thought Catalog Books, an imprint of the digital magazine Thought Catalog, which is owned and operated by The Thought & Expression Company LLC, an independent media organization based in Brooklyn, New York and Los Angeles, California.

This book was produced by Chris Lavergne and Noelle Beams. Art direction and layout by KJ Parish. Special thanks to Bianca Sparacino for creative editorial direction and Isidoros Karamitopoulos for circulation management.

Visit us on the web at thoughtcatalog.com and shopcatalog.com.

ISBN 978-1-949759-07-5

This book was printed in Berlin, Germany with 100% recycled paper and sustainably sourced materials.

I wish you could see yourself through my eyes.

I would show you how beautiful you are, how compassionate you are, how motivated you are, how driven and brilliant and strong you are.

If I could, I would let you see for yourself how optic nerves tingle and delight at the very sight of someone as spectacular and special as you.

I wish I could absorb your pain. I would be a sponge, something you could rely on to help clean up your messes, something you could use to wipe a slate clean.

If I could, I would let your hurt enter my pores, where it would be wrung out and returned to you as love.

I wish I could give you your value in gold. I would raid castles and rob banks and sift mines and steal jewels and leave no pocket unturned.

I would do this if I could, but I can't. You're worth more than the sum of all parts I could collect:

You're worthy of everything.

You are as priceless as you are precious, as brave as you are breathtaking, and there will never, ever be another you.

I know that sometimes it feels like life is only throwing you curveballs and that it can feel lonely to be alone.

I know how badly you want everything to go right, how badly you want someone—not just anyone, but the right one—to go home to at night.

I want you to know that all the difficult shit you're dealing with is only making you a stronger person.

I want you to know that just because your friends are settling down doesn't mean you should settle.

I want you to know what an amazing person you are and that your worth is not defined by anyone else.

I want you to know that you will never have all the answers, and that is ok, because one day you will look back and see how everything fell into place.

Most importantly, I want you to know that you are loved— by me and by many others on your best and your worst days.

You are so precious because you are the only one of you that this world gets to enjoy.

Don't change.

Love,
Me

YOUR SOUL IS A GARDEN.

I hope
you
wake up
smiling
for everything
you have
knowing
it is
enough
right now
you are
enough

It is so
easy
and I will never
let that go
even when you go
my heart will always
have a home
for you

It is ok to not be ok. It is ok to fall apart sometimes, it is ok to have moments with your cheeks pressed to the bathroom tiles, wondering how you got there. It is ok to veer off-course with question marks in your eyes, not knowing where you are going next. It is ok to feel your heart cleave in two, it is ok to wonder how you will put the pieces back together. It is ok to cry until your ribs ache, it is ok to sit with sadness and ask it what it wants. It is ok to say I need you, I'm struggling, lend me your ear, hold my hand.

People paint pictures of perfection because they have been told to live and look and love a certain way. It is ok to not live and look and love like them. Do not compare your reality to their highlight reel, because even though it may not always be apparent, they have days when they are not ok — just like you.

It is ok to feel bruised; it does not mean you are the expired apple in aisle 9 that needs to be discarded. It is ok to feel different; it does not mean you are any less deserving of good things than everyone else. It is ok to ask for help; it does not mean that you are weak and spineless and in a state beyond repair.

It is ok to feel flawed and failed and fearful and confused and broken and lost and let down, and it is also ok to feel nothing at all. These things do not define you. Your goodness and warmth and kindness and compassion and creativity and honesty and heart and every other big and small wonderful thing about you are what define you.

It is ok to not be ok. You will be ok again soon.

We learned in science class
that pressure
makes diamonds
out of coal
there is so much pressure
to be perfect
I don't want to be
a flawless cushion cut
bought from a velvet case
where I was kept on display

I want to be
the sea foam green
smooth center, edges sharp
ocean tumbled piece of sea glass
someone discovers
on the shore
and says, she is imperfect
but she is exactly
what I've been looking for

Look at how far you've come. Look at how much you've grown. If I don't tell you enough that I am proud, I need you to know that I am. If I don't tell you enough that I love you, I need you to know that I do.

You have grown a backbone where your wishbone used to be. You have learned how to say no, you have learned how to walk away. Do you remember when they broke you? It felt like life as you knew it was over. It felt like your rib cage cracked apart. You have rebuilt yourself; you have stitched loss into gain, sadness into joy.

But you, the one who has always loved deeply and fiercely, the one who was always soft; you hardened as you worked brick by brick to make yourself unbreakable.

You don't need to be a fortress to be strong. You don't need to build walls to keep yourself safe. Open the windows and let the breeze breathe life into your bones. Go outside, touch the earth with your bare hands, and remind yourself how it feels to plant the seeds of love and watch them bloom into something beautiful. Water those flowers well; your garden will reawaken in the sun.

I never told you
but I like you
best
when no one else is looking
that is when you finally look
like yourself

Dear body,

I'm sorry for what I did
when I was taking you for granted
these feet
carry me across continents
these legs
help me stand tall
they help me
stand back up when I fall
these arms
wrap around those I love
with the strength of steel
magnolias these shoulders
a place for the weary
to rest their weary heads
these lungs
breathe life into my songs
these ribs
hold the most important part
my strongest muscle
my heart
these muscles, like miracles
can tear and repair
may we always remember
the real reasons they're there

As the sun sets
it also rises
new
as the cold comes
it gives way to warmth
new
as we leave
we will walk back
new
as we say goodbye
there will soon be hello
new

I love you
without hope or agenda
unconditional unplanned unsought
without knowing
how or when or why
yet as certain as
flower seeds assert themselves
deep in my chest
blooming crimson scarlet roses

I love the sunbeams shining
out of your face
hopeful beacons calling lost sea vessels home
from the salt water places I roam
in those ocean eyes
of yours

And if love is pure only
as much as it is sure
then surely I have loved nothing more

I love you
because I know no other way

You looked at me
with the sun in your eyes
and it felt like
coming home

Give thanks for all
that is good and beautiful;
the gifts you carry
people who lift you up
your big, big love
faith and trust that
your life
is unfolding as it should

Give thanks for all
that has been difficult and hard;
trials tribulations tears
tests of self strength fears
all of the unknowns and
days that broke you

Without the darkness
you would not have
learned to
appreciate the light

Climb up into my arms
(tell me the things
you're afraid to say)
it may be autumn, still
I won't let you fall

Dear child,

It's a big, big world out there, and the older you grow, the more people will try to tell you how you should be different. I hope you remember that there are nearly 200 countries on this planet; each has their own ideals of beauty. You will be told you are too much of one thing and too little of something else.

I hope you remember that the first time your mother laid eyes upon you, all she saw was love. The next time you start looking in the mirror at all the things you want to change, I hope you remember that when you came into this world, there were people who looked at you and thought you were the most perfectly formed human they had ever seen. There still are people who look at you and thank the universe each time for giving them such a precious gift. I hope you remember that where you see things you dislike, they see all that is good and beautiful wrapped up in laughter and the things that make you uniquely you.

I hope you always remember that there is no such thing as universal perfection, and to be perfectly imperfect is perfectly good enough.

Maybe I don't despise
winter
maybe I needed
the clarifying cold
to bring important things
into focus
to shed the old
maybe I needed
the warm haze of summer
to be taken away
so that when I
stepped into spring
and turned my face
east to the sun
I would say thank you
instead of
what took you so long?

You were beautiful
before a man said, you are beautiful

You were smart
before a man admired your smarts

You were funny
before a man laughed at your jokes

You were loved
before a man spoke those three words

Sometimes it's hard
to be honest with yourself
but you need your honesty
more than anyone else

We have reached
the end
of the road
there is no map
here
this is where we
fall
this is where we
fly
this is where we
lose ourselves
this is where we
find ourselves
this is where we
end
this is where we
begin again

Every now and then
I invite my ghosts out of the darkness
and into the light
we sit down
they remind me why I loved them once
I guess I always will
they remind me why it's ok
for things to end
I thank them for what they meant to me
and then I let them leave

BEFORE YOU CHEAT, KNOW THIS:

You will break her.
Like the violent shattering of glass as it crashes to the ground.

You will not just break her heart.
You will break her trust.
You will break her spirit.
You will break her joy.
You will break her belief in love.
You will break her sense of self.

BEFORE YOU CHEAT, KNOW THIS:

She will not sleep—not through the night, as she counts the cracks in the walls at 3 am, seeking answers from a God she didn't think she believed in.

She will not eat—not by choice, but because she can't stomach her reality or the thoughts of texts and images that haunt the corners of her mind.

She will not smile—not because there's nothing to smile for, but because she doesn't know what these things are anymore.

BEFORE YOU CHEAT, KNOW THIS:

It will teach her to hear, "You are beautiful" as, "but not beautiful enough." It will teach her to hear, "You are brilliant" as, "but not brilliant enough."

It will teach her to hear, "You mean the world to me" as, "but one person is not enough." It will teach her to hear, "You are the love of my life" as, "but I don't love you enough."

It will teach her to hear, "You are enough" as, "but you are still not good enough to satisfy me."

BEFORE YOU CHEAT, KNOW THIS:

She will cry.

She will sit at her desk until 7:30 pm too embarrassed by tears streaming silently down her face to get up and go.

She will curl into a ball on her best friend's living-room floor, cheek pressed into the carpet—and rather than tell her to get up, he will sit down next to her and say, "I'm here." She will get a lump in her throat anytime she walks past places that used to be yours until she decides to avoid these places entirely.

She will rage.

She will snap at friends, family, and colleagues for no apparent reason. When they are stung by her anger, her cheeks will burn red with shame.

She will curse at her reflection as she's brushing her teeth and think if only she were prettier, funnier, smarter—if only she were more, it would have made a difference.

She will throw a picture frame at the wall and be too dumbfounded to clean the blood off her finger when she cuts it picking up the pieces.

She will scream into the wind by the river, wondering what she did to deserve feeling this way, hoping her words will carry far enough to be heard by someone—anyone—who can tell her.

She will not feel.

She will be turned by shock into the same stone she uses to build walls to keep people out.

She will be numbered in new ways that her hopeful heart had not known to be possible.

And then she will feel everything at once.
She will feel devalued, discarded, disassembled, disillusioned, distraught—she will feel bewildered and betrayed.
She will feel foolish, frenetic, fraught, and full of fear.
She will feel hate—toward you, toward them, toward herself.
She will choke on her own confusion as she tries to hold on yet yearns to let go.

BEFORE YOU CHEAT, KNOW THIS:

She believed in you.
She believed in romance—and that a chivalrous manner meant chivalry in all matters of the heart.
She believed in honesty—and that being honest with your partner first meant being honest with yourself.
She believed in respect—and that a love respected meant not being gaslit nor played a fool. She believed in goodness—and that being good meant working on being good together, even when it was not easy to do.
She believed you would protect her—and that being protected did not mean hiding the truth. She believed in you—and that believing in you, believing in each other, meant the mutual support of a two-person team through the ups, downs, and everything in between.

BEFORE YOU CHEAT, KNOW THIS:

These are all avoidable.
You have a choice.
You can choose to walk away.
You can choose to let her leave on her own accord.
You can give her a choice.

BUT IF YOU CHEAT, KNOW THIS:

You will break her, but she will grow back stronger.

You will dim her light, but she will shine more brightly in the dark.

You will lower her expectations, but she will raise her standards.

You will cause her to hate, but she will find relief, release, and beauty in the breakdown.

You will make her question her sanity, but she will learn to trust her own intuition better than before.

You will crush her ideas of love, but she will never settle again.

You will burn her world to the ground, but she will pour her heart into becoming the best person she can be—and this time, it won't be for you; it will be for her.

Bravery
is not about standing tall
after you've climbed up
the top of a mountain

Bravery
is looking
fear
heartache
rejection
terror
loss
death
in the eye
and saying, "no,
not today"

Bravery
is standing back up
after you've been brought down
to your knees

Hello and

good morning
in case no one has told you
yet today
you are more than ok
and more ok than you think keep
doing what you're doing keep
going where you're going
everything is unfolding as it should
even if you can't see it right now
and most
importantly

You are loved

You are made of mini miracles
you strike awe in someone's heart
you are irreplaceably impressive
you are spectacular as you are

One day, you will encounter someone who is unlike anyone else. The first time you lay eyes upon one another, you will feel like you have known them for years, decades, lifetimes before. You will feel seen as you have never been seen before; you will feel it tingle down your spine, you will feel it in every fiber of your bones.

To meet your mirror is to feel as though you've met yourself residing in another human. As they love you, they will reflect back to you all of the brilliant things you have been failing to celebrate about yourself. As you love them, they will shine light upon your most wicked shadows, the dark places within you that you have been fighting to ignore.

They will show you things that enlighten you and uplift you; they will also show you things that anger you and enrage you. Do not shatter the glass when you don't like what you see. Do not turn away to avoid looking yourself in the eye. This is how you learn.

To find yourself in another person is one of the rarest and most transformational gifts you will ever receive. Treasure them and handle them with care; they will show you the answers you have been seeking. They will show you the way.

Let's get naked
but keep your clothes on

What I mean is —
tell me your secrets
tell me things
no one else knows
tell me what moves you
tell me what
keeps you up at night
tell me your fears
I will protect you
tell me your stories
I will tell you mine

This is the true meaning
of it all
to bare ourselves
with one another
help each other

Love
is the reason

Sunrise is your reminder
that what once grew cold
will begin again new

"What if I am unlovable?" they ask me. "I try so hard, and it never works. I am always left. The ones I want never want me back."

My heart cleaves in two. This person is spectacular, and yet here they are, questioning their worth.

"Listen to me," I say. "Loving the wrong people doesn't mean that you are wrong. Loving people who won't commit doesn't mean that you are not worth committing to. But you cannot give up. There are over seven billion people in this world. You must try and try and try again. Even when you don't want to. Even when you feel like there's no point.

"Look at how many people settle. They settle because they don't want to be alone. They settle because it is safe. They settle because they think they won't have another chance.

"You are not meant to settle. You are one of the special ones. Over seven billion people and only one of you. You are rare. You are a wild, beautiful thing. And just because it is taking longer for you doesn't mean you won't find it.

"Over seven billion people. There is someone who looks at you and thinks you are like art. They think they have never seen someone as magnificent as you. They think everything you touch turns to gold. They think your heart is a place they'd feel safe to call home. They know how special you are. And when they enter your life, they will do whatever they can in their power to make sure you know this.

"There has never before been, and there never will be, another you. You are one of the special ones.

"Don't you ever give up. Don't you ever settle. Don't you ever forget that you are rare."

Before you gave me a home,
you gave me life.

I was born to you, but
before you gave me the world
you gave me a home
within you.

There I lived,
within and then without you—
though you are never far from me.

I carry you within myself
as you once carried me.
I carry you within my heart
always.

I would be a part of nothing today
had I not once been a part of you.

It's not about
fancy shoes
money and fast cars
won't get you very far
it's not about
the way you
look like are you
perfect enough

It's about more like
the strength in your core
knowing you're better today
than you were before
it's not important
to be rich with things
it's important to be
rich
with love
which is the only wealth
that grows the more you
give it away

You grow up thinking
broken hearts will
mend whole
until you realize one day
your heart is full
of holes
from every time you
loved someone
and left a piece
of you
with them

Now I like my hole-filled
heart
it means I loved
hard
and many people I loved
needed that love
more than I did

You are wrong
to think all flowers die
in the winter
roots are there all along
seedlings seeking refuge in the heart
of the earth
waiting for the spring sun
to come back
and say to the dark, you may leave now
it's time to grow

Your soul is a garden
flowers will bloom again
ever hopeful
evergreen

Beauty is
in the eye of the beholder
until you're 13
looking in the
mirror
hearing that
everybody should be beautiful
but not every body is beautiful
unless it reflects XYZ
I wish I could
turn back time
smash every mirror, scale, magazine
but I can't
I just want our sons and daughters
to grow up
differently
than we did

Come walk with me
the way out
is through

You want to know how it all turns out, that you will find your Prince Charming, that you'll be happy and successful and live the kind of life you always dreamed of. You want to know that everything ends up ok, because you're scared of what happens if it doesn't.

You want guarantees, but the thing is: There are no guarantees. There is no master plan that means you're a failure if you don't stick to it. There's no heartbreak-proof love, and there's no surefire way to success. There is no way to block out the bad without blocking out the good. I can't promise you guarantees or all the answers.

What I can promise you is that sometimes the events that derail you will set you on the path to something better. That things might not unfold according to plan, but you'll survive; in fact, you'll come out stronger. I promise that you'll meet people who move you, who make you want to be better, who make you see beauty in things you've never noticed before. I promise that one day you'll wake up, and you will see how everything fell into place to bring you here.

You will finally see how your collection of tiny stories wove together to create this magnificent tapestry that is your life, and it's everything you never knew you always wanted.

There is a story I have written for
all these years
wild bits tangled
broken records on repeat
moments of clarity like glass
love that would make Shakespeare jealous
love that never had a chance
characters walking in and out
for chapters or maybe
just a paragraph or two
tell me
should I have done it any other way
no
this is my story
pages wrinkled and worn
taped back in spots once torn
ripped from the binding
but the spine never collapsed
every word
every plotline
has made me who I am
I love this book

Thank you, winter
for giving me cold
long dark hours
loss grief sorrow
you buried me under
that heavy heart of yours

Thank you, winter
for leading me to
spring
without you
I would not delight so much
in blue skies
and clear intent
but now I can
cast off old coats of burden
turn my face to the sun
and say, kiss me on the nose
you are quite easily my favorite thing

I needed you
spring

Before you turn on your coffee maker
before you confront your concerns
before you tackle your to-do list
before you go to the places you're going

Stop

Pause

Listen

You are doing just fine
everything will work out in time
you deserve to be here
as much as me him they them
and everyone around you
can benefit from the uniqueness that is you
please share it with us
we need it
today

Depression feels like the thick seaside fog rolling ashore from the waves, enshrouding you, blocking your field of vision. It feels like the oppressive humidity on a hot, hot summer day; the air so condensed with water that it feels difficult to breathe. Water: You cannot live without it, yet it can also kill you. Great sweeping tidal waves can crash down upon you out of nowhere; you can drown unexpectedly on the most beautiful day. That is what depression feels like.

Depression will tell you you're not good enough, not attractive enough, not smart enough, not funny enough. Not enough. It will whisper in your ear things you do not want to hear, and you will begin to believe them. It will scream at you. It will laugh in your face.

Depression will come and go as it pleases. It will not discriminate against age or ethnicity, race or religion. It does not care who you are, where you have been, or where you are going. It simply wants to be heard.

I was so ashamed of how strange I felt for so long. I thought that if I could be as beautiful as possible on the outside, it would offset how ugly I felt on the inside. If I could be perfect, if I could be exactly who the world told me to be, I would be loved more, I would matter more. I was wrong. To feel deeply sad is not ugly, after all. Depression is not ugly. It is human. And at the end of the day, we are all human.

Depression can snuff out your flames with one breath. But I slowly discovered that if you can find the strength within you to befriend depression, you will begin to take its power away. Look it in the eye and say, *I do not know why you are here, but I want to learn what you are trying to teach me.* You will begin to draw open the blinds and let daylight enter the darkness and filter its way back into your pores. You will begin to understand that you should not believe everything you think; that every time you told yourself you were unworthy, it was depression speaking to you in lies. You will begin to see how all that is bad has a flip side that is good. That every moment you felt broken down was preparing you to build something better. Shadows grow in the corners we are ignoring, highlighting the spaces that need the most sun.

Please do not give up hope. Depression will not stay with you forever. The most spectacular dawns are born from the darkest of nights; have faith that you will find your way home again.

You can't
make someone
love you
and if you're trying to
you already know
they don't

You can
love you
and if someone
says I love you
too
you will know
they do

The universe
doesn't want you to
feel pain
but when you
feel pain
it is trying
to tell you
how to help
yourself
and each other

Your pain
is not without
purpose
please find
solace
in that

It was only
through
the cracks
that the light
could get in
and reignite
the flames
that had
burned out

The world can be
cruel cold confusing

But look at the full moon
she is whole and shines light
onto even the darkest night
around her
she has the power
to defy gravity and pull tides

You are the moon
don't you forget
your place amongst stars

Don't you
ever
forget
how special
you are
unlike anyone
you are
rare
a wild
beautiful thing

Love a girl who writes
and you must know
you will not be her
entire novel
but you will be
entirely novel
in the things
you teach her
and the places
you go

Love a girl who writes
and you must be ok
with not being the first
to make her pen bleed
her heart onto paper
you might not be the last
but every word
she writes in your name
will be written
only for you

It did not matter
who we were or
where we came from
it did not matter
back then
who we'd become or
where we were going
nothing else mattered
because we had
each other
I will always remember how
we had each other

What if today
was your last day
would you keep
your to-do list
with all its checkboxes
money
degrees
fancy shoes
attention affection
desk job you hate
perfect body perfect face
crumple that paper
throw it away

Find what makes you come alive
find what gives you purpose
go do that
the world needs more people
who have come alive

When you're young
they say you're
weird
and you just want to
belong
they don't say
there's no such thing
as normal
we are all
abnormal
in our own ways
so let your
freak
flag fly
hoist it high
it will keep some away
but it will wave the right ones your way

I love your
weird
it's the best
part about you

Your soul
is a garden
how does
your garden grow

Don't plant perfect posies
all in a row

Sow wildflowers
that reach toward the sky
in brilliant tangles
let your love rain down
and quench them
shine rays of sun
upon yourself
share your
untamed unruly spectacular beautiful
bountiful garden
share your light
with the world

I don't know what inherently triggers us to feel the heart-thoughts of someone else, but I do believe it is coming from something larger than ourselves; a universal, fated design, maybe. I do believe that people come into our lives with a purpose. We are meant to learn from them; we in turn teach them as well. Once the lessons have been imparted, they sometimes continue to stay. More often than not, they go.

The pain of loss will cut you to your core. Your heart will bleed out through your eyes until you feel the crushing weight of loneliness in your chest. But tell me this: Did they inspire you? Did they rekindle the slow-burning fire in you? Did they shake the sleep from you, did they wake you up to the things you've been ignoring?

When they leave, you may feel like you have lost, but the truth is you have gained more than you know. The hole of departure is the place where universal love will flow. Heaven sent you this temporary angel so that you could learn to grow.

When a boy says
you're too smart for him
too good for him
too successful
too much
it is not a compliment
it is an excuse
he wraps up in pretty strings
and beautiful things
to make you feel flattered
enough
while opening it
that you don't notice
he's already walked
out the door

My heart
has gone missing
I don't know where
it could be
plaster it on billboards
flash it on flyers
until it comes back
home to me

HOW TO FAIL:

please everyone
be everything
everyone else wants
you to be
there are seven billion of them
there is one of you

HOW TO SUCCEED:

be yourself
follow your heart
the rest will follow
a few billion won't like it
the ones who matter will

The only true currency
in this precious life
is measured
in how much you love

Maybe it was always supposed to have been you.

Maybe it was always supposed to have been clear.
Maybe it was never really about the chase after all.
Maybe it was never supposed to be the ache of uncertainty,
the waiting on answers. Maybe it was never supposed to
be lying awake with confusion and constantly bathing in
unknowns.
Maybe it was always supposed to have been the crystal
clarity of glass.
Maybe it was always supposed to have been seeing yourself
clearly for who you are and clearly seeing that you are all you
need.

Maybe it was always supposed to have been easy.
Maybe it was hard with those other people for a reason:
because they were not meant for you. Maybe it was never
about convincing someone else that you were good enough;
good enough to be chosen, good enough to want to stay.
Maybe it was never about proving you could win someone
over, even when the odds weren't in your favor.
Maybe it was always supposed to have been walking away
from difficulty and making it easier to choose yourself.

Maybe it was always supposed to have been good.

Maybe you spent years running toward the bad because you were too busy running away from yourself.
Maybe it was never about having to change to please someone else.

Maybe it was never supposed to involve so many disagreements, so many fights, so many ups and downs.
Maybe it was always supposed to have been straightforward and honest; honest-to-goodness, simply good.
Maybe it was always supposed to have been like home.
Maybe it was never about searching the world over, past the most distant shores, combing through sand on your hands and knees, looking for the place you left your heart last.
Maybe it was never about finding someone you hoped would give your weary head and restless limbs a place to finally, finally settle down.
Maybe it was never about finding someone else to give you the home you already have within you.

Maybe it was always supposed to have been like coming home to yourself. Maybe it was always supposed to have been you.

You were born
out of the most complex
combination of
atoms elements helixes genes

You are not here
to be average
you are here
to be extraordinary

Maybe we love
the wrong people
because deep down
we are afraid
of what happens
when it's right

Someone hurt you
it doesn't matter who
your mother
your father
a friend
a lover

Somewhere along the way
you learned what it means
to run fall crack break

Then sometime after that
you learned what it means
to heal rise move past

Tell me
what is stronger than a heart that grows back

I look for you in everyone
half hoping to find you
half hoping I don't

Every time
you have felt
unheard unseen misunderstood scared
I have been there
I will be there again
I will dive in at the deep end
over and over
I will share with you
love loss joy heartbreak
secrets shame mistakes
if that is what it takes

I want you to know:
You are not in this
alone

Wear your heart
on your sleeve
your vulnerability
like a crown
let hope
shine out of your face
like sunbeams

And I promise
there will be no one
lovelier
than you

I want to make
art
out of you
and show it off in
every corner
of the universe
so everyone else
can see
how magnificent
you are

Anyone who ever
made you question that
did not know
true beauty
when they saw it

You are not defined
by the way other people
see you
treat you
love you

You are defined
by the way you
see yourself
treat yourself
love yourself

Others will do unto you
as you teach them how to;
teach them well

Why do you
try so hard
to hold on
to people
who so easily
let you go

There are people
who know your
precious valuable incomparable
worth

They will stay
they will walk
through hellfire
to make sure
you don't get away

The Japanese have a method
of repairing broken things
they take fragments
shards pieces bits
and affix them back
together
with gold

The cracks
gilded in their splendor
make the whole
more beautiful
than it was before

This is the art
of embracing damage
this is recognizing beauty
in broken things

This is me choosing to stay. This is me choosing to try again. This is me acknowledging we are not perfect; you are not perfect, I am not perfect. This is me accepting that we are each made of flaws held together with the glue of good intent. This is me knowing that we have both fallen and failed before, and it may happen again. This is me choosing to get up, dust myself off with one hand, and pull you back to your feet with the other.

This is me choosing to stay. This is me choosing myself. This is me choosing to follow my own heart, my own beliefs. People who care for you will want you to choose what they think is best for you. People who do not care for you will want you to choose what they think is not best for you. This is me understanding that we are each uniquely hardwired individuals, spectacularly distinct humans who think, feel, act, and choose differently. This is me understanding that what feels right for someone else may not also be right for me. This is me accepting that when I choose to stay, other people may not understand, they may think it is wrong— and that is ok.

This is me choosing to stay. This is me choosing love. This is me accepting that when I tried to stop loving you, it felt wrong. This is me knowing that I love you without hope or agenda. This is me giving you my heart without expecting yours in return. This is me understanding that you might break it into pieces; this is me choosing that risk, over and over again. This is me loving you unconditionally; this is me loving you because I know no other way.

This is me choosing to stay. This is me choosing you. This is me seeing you for who you are, not how you look; this is me seeing your awe-inspiring mind, your beautiful heart. This is me understanding that you still may leave. That one day you might get up and go, you might walk away, you might disappear with no explanation. This is me accepting that the choice is yours to make. I cannot beg, borrow, or steal your presence; I cannot keep something that does not want to be kept. This is me knowing that you, and only you, are worth all of these unknowns.

This is me choosing to stay. This is me hoping that you will choose to stay, too.

Isn't it funny
how we keep things
far beyond their expiration date
just to feel
a little less alone
a little more at home?

You are missing
the most important
part
in all of this:

It is ok
to not have all the answers
right now

The sun will still rise
tomorrow

What if
we free these words out loud
what if
we grow
what if
we succeed
what if
we fly
what if
they love us
what if
they stay?

When people always look
at you through idealistic lenses
looking for something from you
looking to take a piece of you home
it will be a shock
the first time someone
sees you
like you're naked
in front of a crowd
bare bones face red and nowhere
to run
it will feel
excruciating and exquisite
at the same time

To be seen
and not looked at
to feel exposed
is how you'll know
they are important
do not let them go

The thing about people
who need to be saved
is you can't save them
unless they want you to

You only have so many
life preservers on board
don't hand them out readily
to people who are reckless
with your heart

Your body
is an intricate network
of tissue and bones
and the blood that breathes
life into your spirit

It carries you
to the places you are going
it absorbs your pain
it shares your joy

Your body
is the vehicle
for the miracle that is you

How can you look
in the mirror
and hate it so?

Trust is not
about having all the answers

Trust is
not having all the answers

And knowing
it is all unfolding
as it should

While you're out there
looking for your big star
remember this:
Chaos and cosmos once came together
in darkness and light
to create this universe
and you

Everything you are searching for
is already right here—
go to your chest
knock on the door of your heart
listen to what you already know

Oceans and mountains
laws of physics and love
dreams and hopes and faith unshakable
the things you want to find
are the very things that make you who you are
the world is in the palm of your hand
waiting for you to
embrace it

You were born to shine.
Not as a faint flicker.
You were born to blaze bright, in all your glory.

You were born to turn your face to the sun and see your radiance looking back at you.

You were born to be a force to be reckoned with, crushing inertia and defying the very laws of physics.

You were born to feel every cell of your body pulsating with all of the promise and possibilities the universe has to offer.

You were born to exist loudly in earth-shattering waves of sound.

You were born to breathe fire at those who constrain and oppress you and do your part in making this world a better place.

You were born to pour your vibrant colors over everything that is black and white.

You were born to channel the stirrings of your soul into existing larger than your physical self.

You were not born to love small.

You were born to follow your heart.
Not with tentative steps.

You were born to chase what makes your spirit sing with reckless abandon.

You were born to turn your face to another and see your tender wild passionate over-the-top romantic respectful honest true love looking back at you.

You were born to risk your own pain for the joy of someone else.

You were born to tear words out of your chest by the teeth of your courage in order to ensure that person won't be the one that got away.

You were born to go down in flames torched upon you by someone you care for deeply in order to be the spring bud peeking its verdant head bravely up toward the sky from these same ashes as you grow back to try again—with someone new.

You were born to cherish and be cherished by a person so phenomenally phenomenal that you dare conceive the idea of conceiving another life together.

You were born to bear gratitude to those you were born to in the same way you will teach your unborn child to bear gratitude to others.

You were born to stare hate in the eye until it cowers under the fortitude of your evil-eradicating compassionate empathetic soft strong all-encompassing open-armed big, big love.

You were not born to learn small.

You were born to walk through shadows and terrors of the night in order to appreciate the light shining out of your chest like stars.

You were born to be destroyed and fractured into strange shapes and unrecognizable pieces in order to discover the power of the glue you use to weld yourself back together.

You were born to wake up one day and look in the mirror, noticing the quiet beauty of your smile and realize that in order to live tremendously and love like it's your last day to live, you had to first learn to love and live for yourself.

"Aren't you afraid you'll fall in love?"

"No.
I fall in love every time I walk out my front door.
I fall in love with people, places, and things.
I fall in love with the way clouds make strange shapes in the sky and the small flower that is brave enough to grow up through a crack in the sidewalk.
I fall in love with a stranger's rare smile on the subway carrying me to work.
I fall in love with people who break me, and then I fall in love with the scars that grow back stronger in their place.
I fall in love with every sunrise I see, because even though I couldn't sleep, it means a new day is just beginning.
I fall in love with words and letters and dog-eared books.
I am not afraid of falling in love.
I am terrified of not falling in love."

Isn't it funny
how something that was once good for us
can become the death of us?

We are only as strong
as the soft parts
we are willing to lay bare on the table.

You are gone now
from me
but not from my heart;
this is where I will carry you
always
this is my promise
to you:

I will not let sadness
grow weeds in the space
you have left behind—
I will use your laughter
to water the flowers
of your big, big love
they will grow there
filling the empty caverns of my chest
they will grow in wild bundles
of joy and eternal spring
they will grow so much
that I will give some away
to other people I love
and then they, too,
will carry you in their hearts.

If
only
we
loved
ourselves
the
way
we
loved
them
imagine
the
mountains
we
could
move

There is no truth
greater
than what you see
when it is just you
and yourself
(if you are willing
to look)

Even kings
drop their crowns
even queens
sometimes fall
the people you think
are perfect
aren't so perfect
after all
they're out there
stumbling
despite giving it
their all
so don't judge
who you've been judging
don't laugh
when they fall

What kind of message
does a man hope to send
a girl he loves
by telling her she is the most
beautiful fascinating exquisite
female
he has ever known
but
he still wants to be with
someone else?

I am all I have left
for me myself
and I
do not want to give
myself
to just anyone
who wants me
I would like to be held very much
in the arms of one man I trust
but I have had too many
arms
carelessly around me
to know when
I will find him

Holding on
to anger
hurts no one
but yourself
it does not
unbreak your heart
it does not
make them come back
it does not
heal

Anger in flames
of white-hot rage will
sit in your chest it will
burn
no one
but you

It is time
to put out
the fire

Just because it went bad
doesn't mean it was never good
just because it turned out wrong
doesn't mean it was never right

I need to give you
credit
for the ways
you enriched my life
for the ways
you helped me grow
for the ways
you made me better

Sometimes I don't want
to look for silver linings
or talk about timing
how things work out
as they should

Sometimes I want to simply
sit down with
rejection
look it in the eye
acknowledge why it's there
without assigning it
some universal meaning
I want to tell it, I wanted that so badly
without hearing reasons
why it couldn't be

It is what it is
it isn't what it never was
and I
am disappointed

Look at this beautiful life you have created.

It belongs to no one else; it is all your own.
You worked so hard to get here.
You fought for what you believed in, even when others
desecrated those same beliefs.
You gave all of your heart to those you loved.
You learned to take your heart back from those who didn't
respect it.

Yes, you have fallen—but you got back up.
Yes, you have hurt others—but you have let their pain teach you.

Look at this beautiful life you have created.
You should be proud.

It is ok to pause every now and then, to truly press pause. In fact, it is absolutely necessary.

Taking a pause does not mean you are missing out, does not mean you are being forgotten, does not mean life is passing you by.

Taking a pause means that you are breathing. It means that you are alive. It means that you are recalibrating to be your best self, that you are stopping to smell the roses you thought had died years ago.

It means that you are tending to the garden of your heart.

Press pause.
Slow down.
Pull the weeds.
Water the flowers.
Breathe.

You are alive.
You are alive.
You are alive.

Strong people can
feel weak and
brave people can
feel afraid and
light people can
feel dark

Lost people can
be found and
hopeless people can
be helped

Keep going
keep going
keep going

It is never too late
to turn things around

You can never tie a string to someone's heart to keep them from walking away; you can only love them in their freedom and hope that they choose to stay, hope that they love you back freely in the same way.

Tell me, what do you believe in
what do you live for
for what would you die
you don't have to be
on your knees
to know what to pray for
you just need to know
how to pray

Love is my religion
I give worship every day
sickness health poverty wealth
sins blessings lies truth
this lifetime a church
and love always the answer
to the questions for which
I pray

Everything felt
cold cruel dark
hopeless helpless hard
and then
there you were
thought I didn't
know it at first
you lifted me
when I needed lifting
you wrapped your arms
around me and
stitched your words
through my heart
you breathed life
back into my broken parts
and when I opened my eyes
it was spring
and you
my endless summer

Sometimes
you look at someone
and never think
of them again

Sometimes
you look at someone
and are never
the same again

It took me years to realize it was not you who had robbed me. I had robbed myself by leaving the door unlocked, giving you my most prized possessions for free.

You are given
so many seasons each year
and every winter
you make it through
to spring
you are given
darkness and cold
so that you may appreciate
the light when it comes

I did not know it then, did not know it until many months or even a couple of years later; in my weakest moment, I was the most strong. Out of my most fragile state, the broken pieces stitched themselves back together from fibers of heartache and steel.

You see, when you feel like your world is ending, when you feel like you are shattered beyond repair and that you will never be ok again, this is where the magic happens.

It is only in your most honest moments, it is only when you feel utterly exposed, it is only when you are stripped bare of everyone and everything that has comprised the construct of who you are that you can truly transform. Observe, learn, grow. You are the only one who can unbreak yourself. It is out of the ashes that your strongest self emerges bright with resolve.

Weak? You were never weak. To be raw is real. To be open is to be courageous. To be vulnerable is to be brave. You turned out to be stronger than you ever could have imagined. Your heart is a garden, and within it blooms strength.

Two people
fall in love
trading secrets fears
hopes dreams
yet they both know
they can never
be together
so they part ways

Love is a victim
of circumstance
tell me
is there anything more
bittersweet
than that?

I hope you do the thing that scares you. We don't grow by carefully avoiding what we fear, circling around it and hoping it will eventually disappear. We grow by walking straight up to it, looking it in the eye and saying, I am here. Show me what you've got. Help me understand why I am afraid of you.

We were hardwired once, many hundreds of years ago, to feel fear as a protective mechanism against perceived threat or pain. Fear says to the gazelle being stalked by lions through stalks of grass: Run. Flee. Survive.

But somewhere along the way, wires got crossed. We began mistaking survival mode for mental and emotional safety. We began building walls around our hearts to stay within our comfort zones. We began believing that not all rewards were worth the risks.

I want to tell him I love him, I say. Fear says, he might leave. I want to try something new, I say. Fear says, you might fail. I want to learn to fly, I say. Fear says, you might fall.

He left. I failed. I fell. It hurt. It hurt. It hurt.

But here's the thing: I am still here. I learned. I grew.

The things we fear—pain, change, heartbreak, loss—are not always comfortable. They frequently hurt. But what breaks us can also build us back stronger.

It has been said that the only thing we should fear is fear itself, and with good reason. Fear will hold you back if you let it. Fear will paralyze you if you let it. Fear will crush your confidence if you let it. Fear will keep you in safety zones— yet fear will also rob you of the most beautiful experiences in life if you let it.

I hope you learn to lean into your discomfort. I hope you do the thing that scares you.

No one
can love you
into feeling whole
that is an inside job
and an unfair task
to ask
of anyone else

You are going to
make mistakes sometimes
veer off your course
do things you've been
trying not to do

It is ok
it is not the end of the world
don't beat yourself up
be more gentle with your own heart
you more than anyone
are deserving of
your love

Actions speak loudly
much louder than words
I love you
means nothing
if it's not spoken
in verbs

Don't show me your
perfect
show me your
broken parts
show me where
they hurt you
when you were young
show me how
they left you
over and over
again
show me your
pain
show me the things
you keep hidden
from daylight
the forgotten places
in your mind

Show me your
cracks
that is where I
will shine your light
show me your
ugly
I will show you
how beautiful
you are inside

Throughout your life,
people will say
you are "too"—

too sensitive
too strong
too emotional
too intense
too trusting
too forgiving
too reserved
too loud
too proud
too nervous
too confident
too driven
too open
too heartbroken
too happy
too mad
too sad
too much

But these are the things
that make you
uniquely, exquisitely you

Ignore the people
who say
you are "too"—

No one ever said
a sunset was too beautiful

They simply said
it was beautiful

ABOVE ALL ELSE,
I HOPE YOU CHOOSE THESE THINGS

I hope you choose kindness. Even when others are being cruel. When someone asks you to give them your heart all warm and full of trust and they give you something makeshift and full of barbed wire in return, be kind. Some people need to feel your heart wrap around them more than you know.

I hope you choose empathy. Even when you don't want to. When someone gives you reasons to judge them, to dislike them, when they behave in ways that you do not understand, be empathetic. Some people need you to walk a mile in their shoes.

I hope you choose calm. Even when you're in the midst of chaos. When someone upends your world and the rest of the world feels utterly upside down, be calm. Some people need you to be their safe haven.

I hope you choose peace. Even when wars rage within and around you. When someone tries to take you to battle, when it feels like your character and choices are under siege, be peaceful.

Some people need your help learning to let go.

I hope you choose trust. Even in the face of falsehoods. When someone has dishonored you, when they have lied to you, when someone has made you feel small, remember that not everyone will do these same things, so be trusting. Some people need you to take leaps of faith.

I hope you choose patience. Even when you are overwhelmed by unknowns. When someone cannot give you answers, when you begin to wonder why you're here, when you simply want to give up, be patient. Some people are truly worth the wait.

I hope you choose love. Even when it would be easier to hate. When someone stirs white-hot rage within you, when they insult you, when they question your worth, be loving. Some people need your love more than you do.

There are many uncertainties in this precious life, but this I am certain of: The people who shine their hearts outward to guide you home safely, the people who put their own hardships aside in order to hand buoys to the hands of those adrift—we need them. The world needs them.

When you're thinking
of someone
and wondering
if they're thinking
of you:
The answer is yes
and no
the truth is
you'll never know
if they don't tell you
they'll never know
if you don't tell them
so speak

Dear fighter,

It is not going to be easy. It is going to be hard, really hard sometimes, but you know in your heart that the best things in life don't come for free, that they require work, they require a fight. You know this because you were not dealt the easy hand of cards when you were young. While other people were given good fortune on a silver platter, you were scraping dreams together on your hands and knees. While other people were told they were perfect and learning that love doesn't have to be earned, you were questioning your value and wondering how the love you craved could be so evasive.

But here is the thing: None of these things make you less than anyone else. None of these things make you less deserving of whatever it is that you want; none of these things make you weaker, or less smart, or unworthy. If anything, these things make you stronger.

People who are dealt the challenging hands are the ones who learn to rise to the challenge. People who have faced struggle and adversity are the ones who know how to best overcome it. People who are broken down are the ones who come back unbreakable; they have seen the worst, and they no longer fear it.

The best people are the ones who have had to fight the hardest. The most interesting people are the ones who are multi-dimensional. The most beautiful people are not defined by a beautiful exterior; they are defined by an open and beautiful heart.

You are going to encounter many people who want to break you down because they don't know how to build themselves up on their own. They will view you as an easy target because you have been broken before. You are going to encounter many people who want to use you and take pieces of you home with them because they think you can fill the holes in their self-esteem that they can't fill themselves. They will view you as an easy target because you have a generous heart.

But none of that matters, because you are you. You are a very strong you, and you are a fighter. You have not gone through what you've gone through to give in now. Your past pains are not without purpose; they are going to help you help other people. You are going to go on to make a wonderful life for yourself, and it will be one that you earned and one that you will be proud of.

You should already be proud of yourself. You have come a long way and you will keep on going. It is not going to be easy, but it is going to be worth it. You are worthy of all of it—remember that.

Stars aren't here to
fade
they're here to burn so
burn
for what moves you
burn for what you love
burn for what makes you better
for what cracks you open

Even if it's just one small thing
find that and make it burn
find that and light it up
maybe you'll light someone else up too
maybe you'll give someone
something to burn for
like you

Brave little bird
with your head in the clouds
betwixt and between
twigs and sticks
this nest you have
outgrown
it is time
to fly but
you are afraid so you
wait wait wait

Dear little bird
please know that
you will be ok
with a little bit of faith
take a deep breath
and leave your tree
even if you start to fall
the wind and your
wings
will carry you

When it feels like you are losing and
everything is going wrong
the sky falls down around you
even birds have lost their song
stop pause breathe
close your eyes
sit in stillness in the dark
listen ever so carefully
open the door to your heart
you will find light there
this invisible yet mighty thing called
hope
is what will give you strength
in weakness
it will give you faith to follow
in uncertainty
hope will
guide you
if you trust it
and hang on

Love is love
is love is love is
kindness compassion compromising
hope faith steadfast surprising
love is respect is love
is love is love is
transcendent trust truth
honesty honor unbiased unconditional
love is breakable love is mendable
love does not see
in colors in shapes in age in
fear in hate in falsehood

love is beautiful
love is for everyone
love takes pride in love

YOU DESERVE to move on.

You deserve to move on from the friends that turned out to not be friends.

The ones who judged you, oppressed you, put you down.

The ones who expected you to think, act, and live the way they do—and made you feel badly when you didn't.

YOU DESERVE to make more room for the people who love you and lift you up.

The ones who support you, celebrate you, motivate you to be better. The ones who would drop everything to be by your side when you need them—even if you haven't seen each other in months.

YOU DESERVE to move on from the love that betrayed you. The one who lied to you, cheated on you, let you down. The one who made you feel like you were crazy—because they couldn't admit their wrongdoings to anyone else, not even themselves.

YOU DESERVE to clear darkness from your heart to create space for someone who will light it up. The one who respects you cares for you, treats you right. The one whose presence amplifies the loving life you already led—and who will be your partner, bringing out your best.

YOU DESERVE to move on from the job that no longer fulfills you. The one that no longer helps you learn, grow, or change.

The one that no longer excites you—because you need to feel like you are living up to a higher potential.

YOU DESERVE *to pursue the passion that drives you. The one that makes you strive, reach, and hope.*

The one that sparks a fire within you—and inspires you to use your skills to help make the world a better place.

You deserve to move on from the home that no longer feels like home. The city that keeps you sleepless, the childhood house that you have outgrown. The place that once gave you joy—but now gives you stress and the sense that something is still missing.

YOU DESERVE to fill your passport and find the home that is all your own.

The countries you discover that are full of interesting people and cultures.

The landscapes and landmarks that open up doors to new opportunities—and open your eyes to new ways of viewing strangers, loved ones, and life.

YOU DESERVE to move on from the past that haunts you.

The memories, experiences, and feelings that hold you back.

The days that turned into months of regret, pain, or sadness—everything that no longer serves you.

YOU DESERVE to move forward in a bright blaze of glory.

Paving your own way, finding your own happiness, making new memories.

Knowing that you, too, deserve everything good and beautiful the world has to offer—and viewing each new day as an opportunity to take these things and make them yours.

YOU DESERVE to be supported.
To be lifted up.

YOU DESERVE to be respected.
To be loved.

YOU DESERVE to learn.
To be challenged.

YOU DESERVE to grow.
To be fulfilled.

YOU DESERVE to discover.
To let go.

YOU DESERVE to move on because you, as much as anyone else, deserve to be happy.

It is time
for you to live
with summer in your bones
to enjoy such
a good thing
for all the rest
of your days

Just because you
have been left
doesn't mean
every person will
leave you

There is no gift more
precious than what
you give yourself
when you finally
let the love you deserve
back in and

I hope you find the
courage
to open your heart wide
once more
let the sun shine inside
let it flood your chest
with every beautiful feeling
you've been denying yourself
you will feel
alive again

Maybe love isn't
first dates and roses
turned church bells and white dresses
turned baby portraits and tall houses

Maybe love is
sights that stun you to silence
your brother sweeping your floor
clean just because he wanted to
someone sweeping you off your feet
into the sand
holding dreams in their hands
before breaking them
and then rebuilding

Maybe love isn't
pretty picture perfect
good better best

Maybe love is
raw rough resilient
tiny moments
without measure

Just because
they don't love you
how you want
them to
does not mean
they do
not
love you
the best way
they know
how

Something they don't teach you
in science
is that the aftershock
is worse
in matters of the heart

The earthquake hits
and just when you've regained
your footing
you're knocked back down
to the ground

Look how far you have come
in just one year:
the mountains you moved
the rivers you forged
the battles you won
to get here

You are braver
than you thought
you are stronger
than you know
you were a force of courage
learning changing letting go
you kept going going going
even when it hurt

That is what
makes you
so damn beautiful

Sometimes sadness washes over me in waves, and with good reason; I can say hello to it, I can understand why it arrived, I can accept that it might linger. Sometimes sadness sets into my bones for no apparent reason at all; it surprises me, it is an uninvited houseguest that won't leave. Sadness feels like a frighteningly cold draft of wind that whips unexpectedly through empty attic windows on a temperate day, sending shivers down your spine, finally settling deep within your marrow.

The curse of feeling deeply is that in order to feel deeply happy, you must also be able to feel deeply sad; you do not get to choose one or the other. When we build walls to keep sadness out, we are also throwing barricades at happiness.

We are conditioned to believe that sadness equates to weakness or instability, and I spent years thinking I was strange, different, wrong. I began avoiding sadness at all costs. Doing so only beckoned winter in further when what I needed was spring. The sun did not return until I broke down my own fortress and learned how to sit comfortably amongst the rubble. Where I saw myself stripped bare by frostbitten failings, you saw promise and beauty evergreen. You stepped around the rocks and planted flowers in my heart. You surveyed my wreckage and loved me anyways.

Happiness and sadness are not so different after all. One is not more weak or strong than the other; one is not more right or wrong than the other. They are both emotional states.

Even in the depths of sadness, there is still the hopeful notion, buried somewhere in the back of my subconscious, that to feel this overcast cannot last. I have walked these familiar roads before, and I know that as things and people come and go, winter will ebb and happiness will once again flow.

Don't let anyone
tell you that you love
too much

You don't love
too much

You just give your big love
to people who love
too small

I want to
crawl between your bones
and sit in your chest
take your heart
in my hands and
tell you how beautiful
it is

The sun
doesn't quit
every time
the moon leaves her

She still rises
the next day
and the next

The sun knows
she was born to shine
she was not born to
give up

Maybe, for the first time, I don't need someone else.

Maybe I am whole without your half.

Maybe whether or not you like the way I look doesn't matter.

Maybe I want to be seen for my mind and humor and sometimes too-large heart.

Maybe I am tired of running from what is good toward what is bad.

Maybe I have learned the value of trust outweighs the value of someone's weight next to me at night.

Maybe I know that my worth is not determined by your desire for me, and maybe I desire nothing less than I am worthy of.

Maybe I understand that being on my own does not make me lonely.

Maybe tomorrow I will meet someone who does not need me, either.

Maybe the point is not that being single makes you free; it's about not giving your love to someone for free when they haven't earned it.

Happiness.

It begins the way the sun rises: a steady spreading warmth that feels like all that is good and gold, increasing in strength as its very light grows stronger. Happiness feels like the onset of spring after a long, bitterly ice-laden winter. It is fitting, then, that we met again in the depths of cold. You came sweeping in with endless summer in your heart and joy in your arms. I was a goner before I knew where we were going. You spoke in birdsongs only I had sung, and I began to believe no other language had ever existed before this.

If joy is a chance burst of feeling and happiness is a constantly existing state, then I don't know where my equilibrium lies on the spectrum. I don't know how to chase joy or capture happiness. I don't know that anyone has the real answers.

But I do know that these happy moments are what make everything else worth it—pain, uncertainty, confusion, grief, sadness. These precious minutes when joy rises sky-high inside of me and eclipses everything else; they are what make life so beautiful.

Yet there is still the haunting notion, buried somewhere in the back of my subconscious, that to feel this elated cannot last. I have walked these familiar roads before, and I know that as things and people come and go, happiness will ebb again as much as it now flows.

It was only through enduring winter that I finally learned:
No matter what cold comes my way, no matter how long
and dark the days may grow—there is hope waiting for me
around the corner.

There is sunlight waiting for me to set it free from within.
There is beauty in breakage, and there is love after loss.

It was only through enduring winter that I finally learned
how to find my endless summer.

KIRSTEN ROBINSON is a writer who began fearlessly baring her heart in a raw, relatable and inspirational way under the social media pseudonym Naked Writing. She believes that writing and creative expression can be powerful tools for supporting people in healing and processing daily life. Through poetry and prose, she hopes to help others feel less alone in their own journeys of love, loss, and personal growth—providing the same sense of comfort that she herself has found in reading since childhood. She is currently based in New York.

instagram.com/nakedwriting
www.facebook.com/nakedwriting